Cows

by Peter Brady

W
FRANKLIN WATTS
NEW YORK • LONDON • SYDNEY

This edition first published in 1998

Franklin Watts
96 Leonard Street
London EC2A 4RH

Franklin Watts Australia
14 Mars Road
Lane Cove
NSW 2066

Original edition published in the United States by Capstone Press
818 North Willow Street, Mankato, Minnesota 56001
Copyright © 1996, 1998 by Capstone Press

ISBN 0 7496 3201 1
Dewey Decimal Classification Number: 636.2

A CIP catalogue record for this book is available from the British Library.

Printed in Belgium

Photographs
All the photographs were taken by William Muñoz.

Contents

Words in the text in **bold** type are explained in the Useful words section on page 23.

What is a cow?

A cow is a farm animal.
Cows are female **cattle**.
Male cattle are called bulls.
Dairy cattle give us milk.
Beef cattle give us meat.

What cows look like

Cows have large, heavy bodies
and a long tail.
They have an **udder** that holds milk.
Cows can be black, white,
different shades of brown, or spotted.
Cows can weigh between 450 and
1,350 kilos.

Where cows live

Cows live mostly in herds, without bulls.
In the summer farmers keep cows
in fields of grass called **pastures**.
In winter farmers usually
bring their cows into barns
for warmth and shelter.

What cows eat

Cows eat grass, hay, clover
and special cattle food.
Cows have four stomachs,
but no top front teeth.
They drink over 76 litres of water
every day.

Chewing the cud

Cows swallow their food more than once.
First they chew it until
it is soft enough to swallow.
Later they bring the food up
and chew it again.
This is called chewing the **cud**.

Different kinds of cow

Farmers have kept cows
for hundreds of years.
Now there are more than
250 different **breeds** of cow.
The names of some of them are Jersey,
Guernsey, Aberdeen Angus, Hereford,
Charolais, and the well-known
black-and-white Friesian.

Milking

Dairy cows, which give us milk,
are milked twice a day.
Some breeds produce
more milk than others,
but most dairy cows give up to
23 litres of milk a day.
That is about 100 glasses of milk.

Calves

Cows have one calf a year.
They are pregnant for nine months
and give birth in the spring.
A female calf can become a mother
in about two years.

What cows give us

Cows give us milk.
Milk is used to make dairy products,
such as butter, cheese,
yogurt and ice-cream.
Cows give us meat for beefburgers,
mince, steaks and roast beef.
Cows' skins are made into leather
for shoes, clothes and furniture.

Make your own butter

What you need

$\frac{1}{4}$ litre whipping cream
small glass jar with a screw-top

What you do

1 The cream must be at room temperature, so take it out of the fridge an hour before you start.
2 Put the cream into the jar. Screw the lid on tightly and shake the jar well. In about 10 minutes lumps of yellow fat will start to form.
3 Keep on shaking until there is a large lump of butter.
4 Empty the jar into a bowl and pour off the liquid. This is buttermilk.
5 Gently rinse the butter with water until there is no more buttermilk.
6 Press the butter against the side of the bowl with a wooden spoon.
7 Stir in a little salt.

Now the butter is ready to taste and use.

Useful words

breed   group of animals with the same ancestors

cattle   the word to describe all bulls, cows and calves

cud   food brought up from one stomach to be chewed again

pasture   a field with grass and other small plants for cows to eat

udder   the bag under a cow that holds its milk

Books to read

Baker, Susan, *Dairy Foods and Drinks,* Zoe Books, 1997
First Discovery: Farm Animals, Moonlight Publishing, 1996
McKenzie, Sarah, *On the Farm*, Wayland, 1985
See How They Grow: Calf, Dorling Kindersley, 1993

Index

PRINTED IN BELGIUM BY
proost
INTERNATIONAL BOOK PRODUCTION